PLAYING GOSPEL PIANO

The Basics

With Examples from
Lift Every Voice and Sing II

Carl MaultsBy

CHURCH PUBLISHING INCORPORATED

Text copyright © 2003 by Carl MaultsBy. All rights reserved.

"God is Love" copyright © 2003 by Carl MaultsBy. All rights reserved.

"Come with us, O blessed Jesus," from *The Hymnal 1982* copyright © 1985 by The Church Pension Fund. Used by permission. Stanzas 2 and 3 © The Estate of Charles P. Price. Used by Permission.

All selections from *Lift Every Voice and Sing II* copyright © 1993 by The Church Pension Fund. Used by permission. The arrangement of "This Little Light of Mine" © Horace Clarence Boyer. Used by Permission.

Every effort has been made to trace the owner or holder of each copyrighted selection used in this book. If any rights have been inadvertently infringed upon, the Publishers ask that the omission be excused and agree to make the necessary corrections in subsequent printings.

Church Publishing Incorporated
19 East 34th Street
New York NY 10016

ISBN-13: 978-1-64065-545-4 (paperback)

To the memory of the late Melita D. Wright, my first piano teacher, who taught me how to add "some extra" when playing hymns.

CONTENTS

Acknowledgments vii

Resources for Gospel Music in Print viii

Playing Gospel Piano: The Basics 1

Touch Me, Lord Jesus 21

Lift Him Up 22-25

Near the Cross 26-29

On Christ the Solid Rock 30-31

Come, Ye Disconsolate 33-35

When We All Get to Heaven 37-39

We're Marching to Zion 40-41

This Little Light of Mine 42-43

There Is a Fountain 44-45

Leaning on the Everlasting Arms 46-49

Jesus, Lover of My Soul 50-58

God Is Love 59-67

ACKNOWLEDGMENTS

Thanks to the following who assisted me in the preparation of this manual:
Marilyn Haskel
Valerie Pyfrom
Aleece Carson
Marvin Curtis
Sharon Heyward
Portia Maultsby
E. R. Shipp
Howard Begun

My eternal gratitude to all my teachers of piano and music theory, but especially:
Ann D. Bowen
Edna Hargrett Thrower
the late Robert Huhn
Charles Smith
the late Lessie Brayboy Weaver
James W. Wilson

RESOURCES FOR GOSPEL MUSIC IN PRINT

Mr. David Reid, *Owner*
Reid's Music-Berkeley
3181 Sacramento Street
Berkeley, CA 94702-2723
Telephone: 1-510-843-7282
Fax: 1-510-644-80381

Ms. Willie Eva Smith, *Owner*
Dekays' House of Music
San Francisco, CA
Telephone: 1-415-239-8471

Mary Bonner, *Administrator*
Burleigh workshop & Ministry, Incorporated
PO Box 16091
Oklahoma City, OK 73113
Telephone: 1-405-842-3470

N-Time Music
http://www.ntimemusic.com

Black Gospel Music
http://www. Blackgospel. Com/marketplace/sheet/smptitles.asp

Brooklyn Tabernacle Bookstore
http://www.brooklyntabernacle.org/bookstore/category.cfm?cID=19&x=22&y=5

PLAYING GOSPEL PIANO: THE BASICS

More and more gospel music is finding its way into liturgical and other mainline worship services. Gospel music in worship is growing by leaps and bounds. It is not just a passing trend. In some quarters, gospel music has been met with resistance. However, most of the resistance to gospel music in worship generally comes from persons who are not familiar with gospel music's stylistic traditions, its beauty, or its emotional and spiritual impact.

Until recently, this music was notated with a sketch or outline of the vocal melody, together with basic harmonic progression. The same is true of the instrumental accompaniment. It was assumed that both the singer and the accompanist would be versed enough in the style to supply the missing detail. Therefore, the best way for a keyboardist to learn the style was through listening to other gospel musicians and to their recordings, and imitating their playing until the keyboardist was able to put his or her personal stamp on the music.

At a recent conference on sacred music, I was asked to lead a workshop on the use of gospel music in the liturgy. After hearing me give a brief history of gospel music, presenting many examples of gospel-style service music and anthems keyed to the liturgy, one attendee lamented, "How am I supposed to learn to play this music if it's not written, and if, when it *is* written, it's not complete?" The answer to that remains: *imitation is best*. But there are a few basic rudiments of the gospel keyboard style that, with a little ingenuity, can make the most elementary keyboardist sound like a proficient gospel musician. This book contains several examples of hymns as written and as played.

Historical Perspective

To play gospel, it is helpful to understand a bit of its history. While William Henry Sherwood's "Mountain Top Dwelling" was published in 1883 and Charles Price Jones's "Where Shall I Be When the First Trumpet Sounds?" was published in 1899, Thomas Andrew Dorsey is given much of the credit for shaping and developing early African-American gospel music.[1] His first gospel composition, "He'll Know Me Over Yonder," was published in 1930. Until his "reconversion to Christianity", Dorsey was a "blues and ragtime piano man for Ma Rainey."[2]

Three figures emerge as the leading examples and most influential keyboardists in early traditional gospel music: Clara Ward of Philadelphia and the team of Roberta Martin and Lucie E. Campbell of the Roberta Martin Singers of Chicago. Ward and Martin were protégées of Dorsey. The Roberta Martin Singers were generally accompanied by Martin on piano and Campbell on the Hammond organ.

Although a Baptist, Clara Ward translated the drum and tambourine rhythms of the Holiness Church into piano figures. Her style was more percussive than lyrical. Ward was said to "tear-up a piano" (African-American church lingo for playing a piano extremely well and with a lot of fire).

On the other hand, Roberta Martin, a pianist trained in the classical conservatory technique, played in a more restrained style. With the chords concentrated in the lower middle piano register, she used a driving rhythm figure that alternated between a principal chord and a chord that was a diatonic second higher. Martin's style defined what I call the "Baptist shuffle" (see *Example 1*).

---

[1] Boyer, Horace, "'Take My Hand, Precious Lord, Lead Me on,'" in *We'll Understand It Better By and By*, ed. Bernice Reagon, p. 142. Smithsonian Institution Press, Washington and London, 1992.

[2] Quote by Thomas Dorsey in 1982 film *Say Amen, Somebody*.

Example 1 *The Baptist Shuffle*

The music of Dorsey and other early proponents of gospel music reflects a synthesis of African-American musical traditions: chant, spirituals, blues, and jazz. All of these styles are rooted in African performance practice. Hence, the rhythmic element is of utmost importance, especially in the accompaniment.

In contrast, European and Western-based music emphasizes the melody. Harmony and rhythm are subordinate. In an African-based music such as gospel, even the melody tends to be rhythmically connected. For example, a singer may vamp—i.e., repeat a figure an unspecified number of times—for minutes on a simple phrase such as "Oh, Jesus" simply because of a hypnotic quality created by the rhythm of the words.

Gospel and Blues

Gospel and blues have always been intertwined. Harmonically, both forms rely heavily on dominant seventh chords. Many of the melodic lines are interchangeable between the sacred and the secular blues. Structurally, they are different. Whereas the primary chord progression of the secular blues has emerged into a set form of twelve bars which follows the basic progression $I^7|\ I^7|\ I^7|\ I^7|\ IV^7|\ IV^7|\ I^7|\ I^7|\ V^7|\ IV^7|\ I^7\ |I^7$, the gospel blues format is not as crystallized. More often than not, the gospel blues is 16 bars or longer in structure.

Lucie E. Campbell's "Touch Me, Lord Jesus" *(see page 21)* is an excellent illustration of a gospel blues. Although its originally published hymn-like setting belies the song's blues character, the recording by the Angelic Singers of Philadelphia became the definitive rendition and left little room for doubt of the blues influence. The structure of "Touch Me, Lord Jesus" is I|IV, IV^7|I|IV| II^7 (major) |V^7|I, IV/I, I|V^7| V^7|I|IV|I|I/V, II (major), V^7|I. Moreover, this example is representative of how a fair amount of early traditional gospel was disseminated in print.

Rhythmic Features found in Gospel

Meter

Because of its African roots, most traditional gospel music has an underlying triple feel, even when it is in duple meter. Therefore, the music, as in blues and jazz, tends to have either a 6/8, 9/8 or 12/8 feel. In their book *West African Rhythms for Drumset,* Hartigan, Adzenyah and Donkor write:

> Remember that notation in 12/8 and 4/4 is a western musical concept. While these time signatures are helpful in learning to play them, West African and Afro-Caribbean music do not structure time in such a pronounced manner. One of the many beauties of these traditions is the blurring of duple/triple distinctions in performance....[3]

Similarly in gospel music, duple/triple distinctions are often blurred or at best intertwined.

Example 2: *The Baptist Shuffle, written and played*

For example, the fast gospel-shout style is written in 4/4; however, it is traditional for it to subdivide at key points into a triple feel, thereby creating a sense of 12/8 rhythm.

Those students of classical western music will recognize this principle of subdivision or secondary meters from the writings of J. S. Bach. In the hymn chorale "Jesu, Joy of Man's Desiring," Bach transforms Johann Schop's original square 3/4 time hymn tune into a flowing masterpiece in 9/8 time. (See *Examples 2a and 2b*.)

---

[3] Hartigan, Royal with Adzenyah, Abraham and Dnokor, Freeman, *West African Rhythms for Drumset,* ed. Dan Thress, p. 65. Manhattan Music, Inc. (Administered by Warner Bros. Publications Inc.), Miami, FL, 1995.

Example 2a

Come With Us, O Blessed Jesus *(The hymn as written; transposed for use with Example 2b)*

Words: John Henry Hopkins, Jr.
Charles P. Price

Music: *Werde munter*, Johann Schop
arr. and harm. Johann Sebastian Bach

1. Come with us, O blessed Jesus, with us ever more to be; and though leaving now thine altar, let us nevermore leave thee. Be thou one with us for ever, in our life thy
*2. Come with us, O mighty Savior, God from God, and Light from Light; thou art God, thy glory veiling, so that we may bear the sight. Now we go to seek and serve thee, through our work as
*3. Come with us, O King of glory, by angelic voices praised; in our hearts as in thy heaven, be enraptured anthems raised. Let the mighty chorus ever sing its glad ex-

4

Example 2b

Jesu, Joy of Man's Desiring
(The hymn chorale)

J. S. Bach

+ Chorale Melody

In *LEVAS II*, hymn 105, "I'm So Glad Jesus Lifted Me," is a perfect example of this duple/triple obscuration (see *Examples 3 and 4*).

Example 3: I'm so Glad Jesus Lifted Me *(The hymn as written)*

Example 4: I'm so Glad Jesus Lifted Me *(The hymn as played)*

8

The Repeated Note

The repeated note is another example of the rhythmic component of gospel music. In the early days, gospel was more often than not played on substandard, untuned pianos with keys that did not easily sound. This resulted in the keyboardist playing a series of rapidly repeated notes on a single key (usually the tonic or the dominant of the song's tone center) to insure the sounding of the note (see *Example 5*).

Example 5

Initially a performance necessity, but now a stylistic practice, the repeated-note figure has another interesting history that arose out of gospel piano accompanying techniques. Often times a vocalist would start singing a cappella without advising the pianist of the key of the song. It was then the job of the pianist to find the key and accompany the singer. Inasmuch as most accompanists did not have perfect pitch, the repeated note was used as a means of reassuring the pianist and the singer that they were in the same key. Today the repeated note, generally played in a sixteenth triplet rhythm, is a standard motif in gospel keyboard accompaniment.

Metric Transformation

A typical rhythmic feature of African-American gospel music is the practice of taking a 3/4 meter hymn and performing it as a 12/8—hence, a four-beat pulse. This gives the music both a duple and triple feel at the same time. Triple meter in the form of a Western-waltz time is eschewed in gospel. For example, let us examine how the J. J. Husband hymn "Revive Us Again" (*LEVAS II,* hymn 157) is transformed:

Example 6: *The hymn as written*

Revive Us Again
Words: William P. MacKay

Music: John J. Husband

Revive Us Again
Lyrics: W. P. McKay

Music: J. J. Husband

Example 7

Revive Us Again
(The hymn as played)

Piano Pedals as Drums

As a further illustration of the importance of the rhythm in gospel music, consider the historical use of the piano pedals.

Many churches did not and still do not use drums in worship services. Sometimes this omission was attributed to religious dictums, a carryover from the seventeenth-century ban on African slaves playing drums. At other times, drums simply were not available.

Since it was a lucky day when the gospel church piano's sostenuto pedal sustained properly or the una corda pedal indeed made the piano softer, the pedals were often relegated to the role of a bass drum-like, time keeper. This effect was achieved by the "thump" sound the pedals made against the baseboard when the pedal was struck hard and released. Fortunately, today this is not the norm; and this stylistic component has disappeared.

Other Influences Shaping Rhythmic Accompaniment

The influence of the African chant on gospel music is best seen in the vocal styling. However, the rhythmic drum accompaniment figures associated with the chant became an integral part of gospel piano accompaniment. Moreover, the crucial factors that shape the rhythm of a gospel-style keyboard accompaniment are meter, tempo, basic chord progression, and melody.

The melody and chord progression go hand in hand in determining which of the following functional harmonic chords are to be used: appogiatura or leaning chord, passing chord, leading chord (see *Example 8*).[4]

A fast gospel shout (see *Example 1*) will use more appogiatura chords than a gospel ballad; similarly, a gospel ballad (*e.g., LEVAS II*, hymn 214, "God Is So Good") is likely to use more passing chords than a gospel shout. Nevertheless, it is the underlying rhythm that gives a gospel composition its character.

We have seen in Example 1 the use of the passing chord as an integral element of the basic shout rhythm. Similarly, passing and leading tones in octaves are used in the bass as a connector from one chord in a progression to the next (see *Example 8*).

Example 8: *Functional harmonic chords*

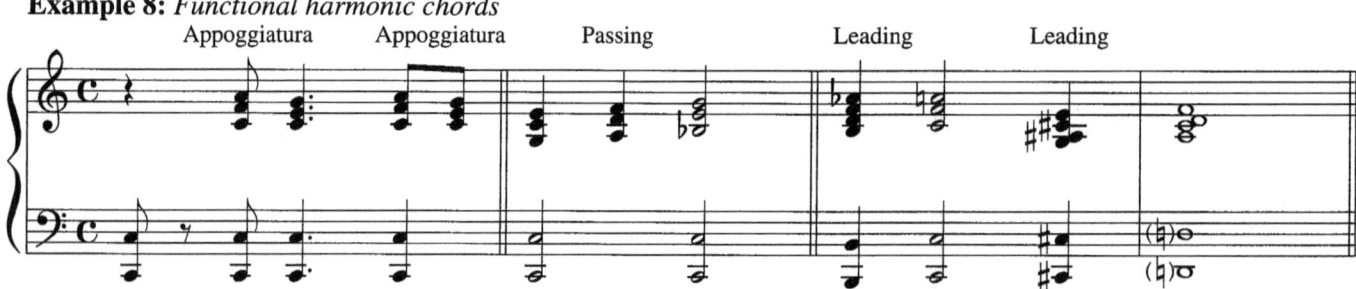

In the playing of Ward, Martin and Smith, the driving left-hand bass was an integral part of the technique. Usually, the left hand played in octaves. A stylistic feature that is used in today's playing. Because of gospel music's roots in early jazz—principally ragtime and blues—the left hand of the piano often imitated a string bass line in which the root of a chord alternated with the fifth of the chord (see *"I'm So Glad Jesus Lifted Me," Example 3*.) In slower moving passages, the left hand played more in the stride style: the root of the chord in octaves followed by the chord (see *Example 9*).

---

[4] These terms correspond to terms used to characterize non-harmonic tones in conservatory basic theory analysis of a melody; the chords also function similarly.

Example 9: *Left Hand in "Stride" style*

However, as is often the case in jazz vocal accompaniment, chords are voiced so that at any given time the highest note in the chord is the same as a corresponding note in the melody (see *Example 10*).

Example 10: *Melody line with melody in upper voice of chords in the piano*

However, the most popular and perhaps most infectious bass accompaniment is the chromatic-bass shout pattern (see *Example 11*). This pattern is often played as an "Alberti" (also known as a "Boogie") bass pattern as shown in *Example 12*.

Example 11: *Chromatic bass shout pattern*

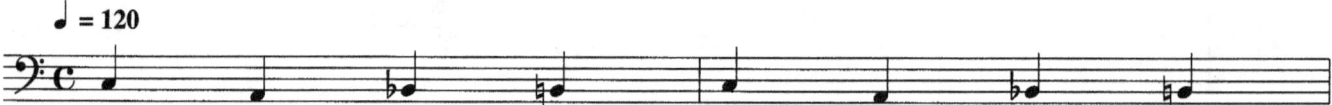

Example 12: *Alberti/Boogie chromatic bass pattern*

The leading contemporary heir to these styles is Richard Smallwood of Washington, D. C. Smallwood did for gospel piano playing what Beethoven did for the classical sonata form: he extended it to the point that it became an almost new entity unto itself. His solo piano treatment of Albert Hay Malotte's "The Lord's Prayer"[5] and "Blessed Assurance"[6] incorporated conservatory concertato-styled figures with gospel figures and contemporary popular piano figures.

The Gospel Ballad

The term "gospel ballad" refers to music in the gospel idiom that is performed at a slow tempo or in free, recitative-like style. Unlike historical European folk ballads in which the form of the text is dictated by a set number of rhyme schemes, the gospel ballad text may follow a particular rhyme scheme, but often it is improvisational in manner and may not follow a rhyme pattern, preset or otherwise.

Gospel Fills (Licks)

Standard gospel fills, which provide the music necessary to complete or "fill up" a measure at the end of a phrase, are derived from performance practices. One was the playing of tunes in keys of four or more flats. For example, Clara Ward's favorite key was A Flat. Since many of the early gospel piano players were not proficient in reading music, they, unlike many of their musically literate counterparts, were not afraid to play in tonalities such as D Flat (C Sharp), G Flat (F Sharp) and B (C Flat) Major. In fact, gospel pianists preferred these tonalities because the keyboard conformed more easily to the shape of the hands.

---

[5] The Richard Smallwood Singers, "The Lord's Prayer," track 5 of the CD *Recorded Live at Howard University*, Sparrow Records 1352.
[6] "Blessed Assurance," track 7 of the CD *Portrait*, A&M /Word CD 75021 84692.

Therefore, one favorite gospel fill is a descending pentatonic scale based on a minor chord with a dominant seventh and suspended fourth played in a triple feel (see *Example 13*). Of course, over the years this lick has been transposed and varied (see *Example 14*); but it essentially retains its punch in any key.

Example 13: *A Pentatonic Fill*

Example 14: *Variation of a Pentatonic fill*

The I-V fill is another popular lick used at the end of verses:

Example 15: *I-V fill*

Gospel Chord Progressions and Vamps

Perhaps the most popular progression in gospel music is the I – IV – I (see *Example 16*).

Example 16: *[I-IV-I Progression]*

A tonic chord in the second inversion (called either a "I^6_4" or a "I/V" chord) is found so often in gospel that any piece that uses it, especially on a piano, at any strategic point in the composition or with any regularity, is going to suggest a decidedly gospel influence. Frequently, this chord is used as a substitute for a dominant 7th chord. Two favorite gospel progressions on which keyboardists and singers vamp *ad infinitum* are the I^6_4 – VI (see *Example 17*) and the I^6_4 – IV (see *Example 18)*.

These progressions as vamps are found more in solo and choral than in congregational hymn accompanying. Their use immediately heightens the emotional moment.

Example 17: *[I^6_4-VI Progression]*

Example 18: *[I^6_4-IV Progression]*

Gospel and the Pipe Organ

A large number of churches throughout the world are designed so that the pipe organ is the only instrument available in either the chancel, the gallery, or any other location in the worship space. Although targeted for piano, the principles outlined in this manual are for the most part transferable to the pipe organ or to any other keyboard. A few minor modifications are necessary.

In the treble manuals, use only flute 8' and 2' stops. On some organs, certain 4' flutes may be used as long as they don't obscure the sound of the 8'. This combination will give the effect of a Hammond organ, the second most widely used keyboard instrument in gospel. When the tempo is not too bright, left-hand bass passages written in octaves should be played as single notes in either the pedal or on a separate manual which uses a fat 16' foundation stop combined with flutes 8' and 16'. If the organ is in a very reverberant room, play fast passages as detached as possible.

Contemporary Gospel (1968-1998)

The discussion to this point has focused on playing in the "traditional gospel" style. To its credit gospel has always been an eclectic music. It readily accepts influences from various sources—e.g., jazz, reggae, classical conservatory. With the release in 1968 of the Edwin Hawkins recording of "Oh Happy Day" from the album *Let Us Go Into the House of the Lord*, gospel music began a new era: contemporary gospel.

As mentioned earlier, an attribute of African-based music is the lack of distinction between the sacred and the secular. "Oh Happy Day" is a perfect illustration of this concept. On this track and throughout the album, Hawkins fused the sacred traditional gospel/hymnody with secular sixties rhythm and blues (r&b) riffs (a short repeated melody of 2-4 bars in length) and rhythm patterns. In addition, he introduced chords that used the upper harmonics of 9ths, 11ths, 13ths. This paved the way for the introduction of bi-tonality and other musical elements that had previously existed only in the realm of jazz and conservatory-based compositions. The result was an unqualified commercial success. Over the last three decades, the album has sold more than 7million units. "Oh Happy Day" created an unprecedented interest and accelerated growth in the appeal of gospel music.

Another track from the *Let Us Go Into the House of the Lord* album is Hawkins' version of "Jesus, Lover of My Soul." The text, like "Oh Happy Day" is based upon an 18th century hymn (see example 31a). Contrast the hymn setting of "Jesus, Lover of My Soul" with the Hawkins tune (see page 52).

In the late sixties and the early seventies, the evangelical "Born Again" Christian (BAC) movement swept the nation and claimed a fair number of rhythm and blues/pop/disco artists as converts—most notably, Al Green and Donna Summer. Not unlike Thomas A. Dorsey before them, these BAC proselytes took their secular music idioms, combined them with sacred texts, and performed them in Christian sanctuaries instead of—and in the case of Summer—in addition to, concerts and sports arenas.

Nouveau Gospel (1998-)

In 1998, gospel artist Kirk Franklin released an album, *Kirk Franklin and the Family*, which included the track "Why We Sing." The commercial impact of this track was reminiscent of the success of "Oh Happy Day" three decades earlier. Within the first year of its release, *Kirk Franklin and the Family* sold in excess of a million units. In addition to its marketing success, this album made it possible for a 1997 recording by Franklin and the group billed as "God's Property" to have a major crossover gospel hit single, "Stomp." "Stomp" is significant because it reflected an unabashed fusion of gospel and the rhythms of "hip-hop," a secular music that was an outgrowth of "rap" music. The music is quite syncopated and built upon a few riffs, usually in the bass. Although the piano is still used, the keyboard instrument of choice tends to be the synthesizer. Often when a piano sound is preferred, the sound is a synthesized or sampled piano.

As r&b, hip-hop, and other secular styles exerted greater influence on gospel, publishers of this sacred music genre followed the lead of their secular counterparts (see page 59, as an example), and printed and distributed note-per-note sheet music transcriptions of contemporary and nouveau gospel recordings. As a result, the music is more accessible to larger audience. Because nouveau gospel is now so widely available in print, it is not within the purview of this discussion. Thanks to the Internet, copies are bought overnight, rehearsed by the local choir on Thursday evenings, and sung in worship on Sunday morning.

Although the debate about the appropriateness of gospel music in worship is less widespread, the debate in some quarters is no less intense than in the early days of Thomas A. Dorsey. In the twenty-first century, the whole spectrum of gospel music from traditional to nouveau is valid for inclusion in worship if it satisfies the following two conditions: is it good—i.e., is it presented with integrity, and does it enhance the word of God? God is good and all good things come from God.

Touch Me, Lord Jesus Music: Lucie E. Campbell

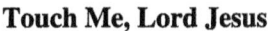

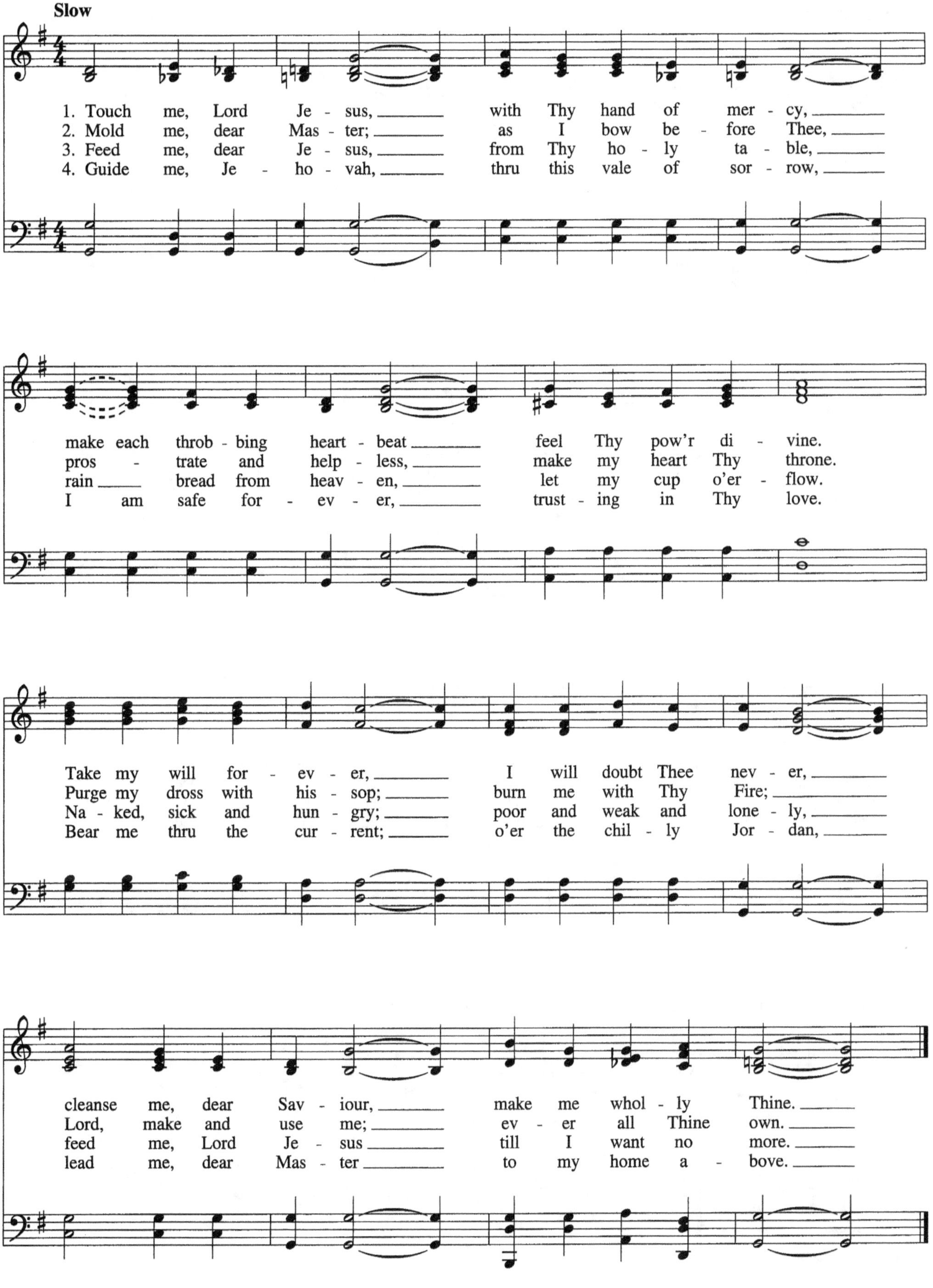

Lift Him Up *(The hymn as written)*

Words: Johnson Oatman, Jr. Music: B. B. Beall

1. How to reach the mass-es, those of ev-'ry birth, for an an-swer Je-sus gave the key; "And I, if I be lift-ed up from the earth, will draw all men* un-to Me."
2. Oh! the world is hun-gry for the liv-ing bread, lift the Sav-ior up for them to see; trust Him and do not doubt the words that He said, "I'll draw all men* un-to Me."
3. Don't ex-alt the preach-er, don't ex-alt the pew, preach the gos-pel sim-ple, full and free; prove Him and you will find that prom-ise is true, "I'll draw all men* un-to Me."
4. Lift Him up by liv-ing as a Chris-tian ought, let the world in you the Sav-ior see; then all will glad-ly fol-low Him who once taught, "I'll draw all men* un-to Me."

Lift Him up, _____ lift Him up, _____
Lift the pre-cious sav-ior up, lift the pre-cious sav-ior up,

* "folk" may be substituted for "men."

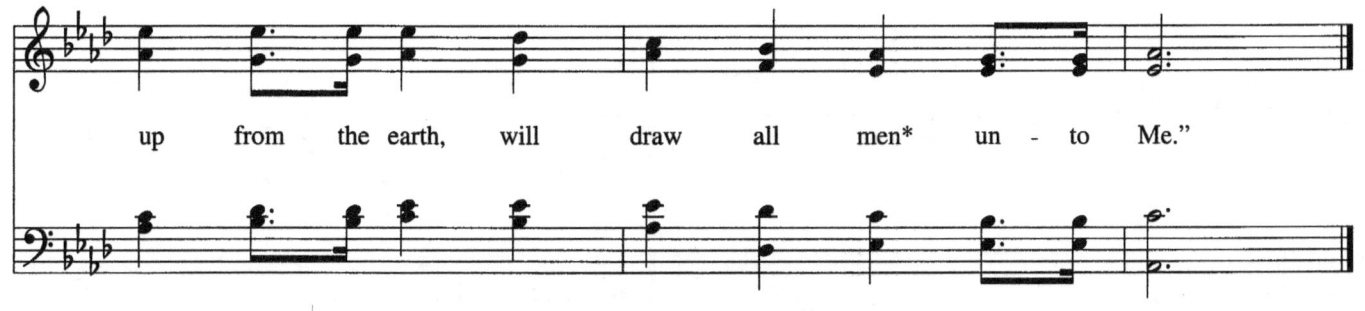

Lift Him Up
(The hymn as played)

arr. Carl MaultsBy
© 2001 Malted Milk Music

Near the Cross *(The hymn as written)*

Words: Fanny J. Crosby　　　　　　　　　　　　　　　　　　　　　　　　Music: William H. Doane

1. Jesus, keep me near the cross, there's a precious fountain;
2. Near the cross, a trembling soul, love and mercy found me;
3. Near the cross! O Lamb of God, bring its scenes before me;
4. Near the cross, I'll watch and wait, hoping, trusting ever,

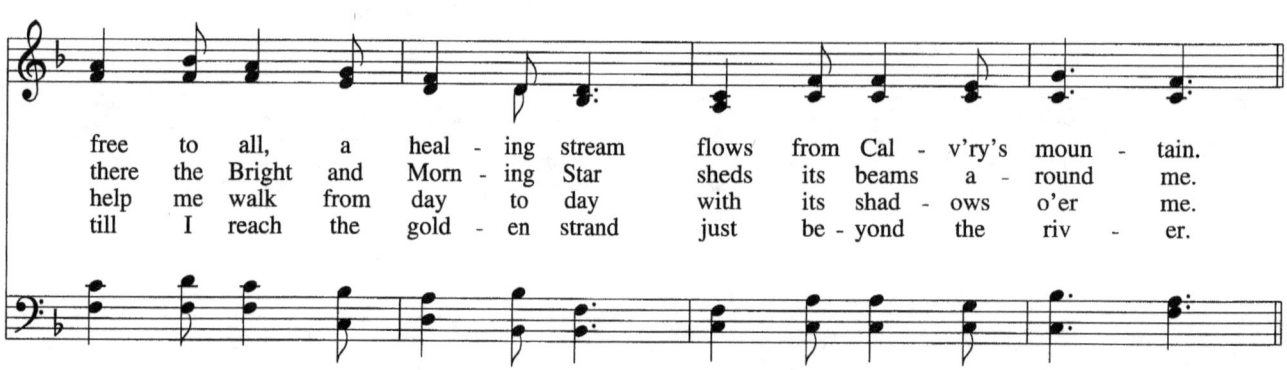

free to all, a healing stream flows from Cal-v'ry's mountain.
there the Bright and Morning Star sheds its beams around me.
help me walk from day to day with its shadows o'er me.
till I reach the golden strand just beyond the river.

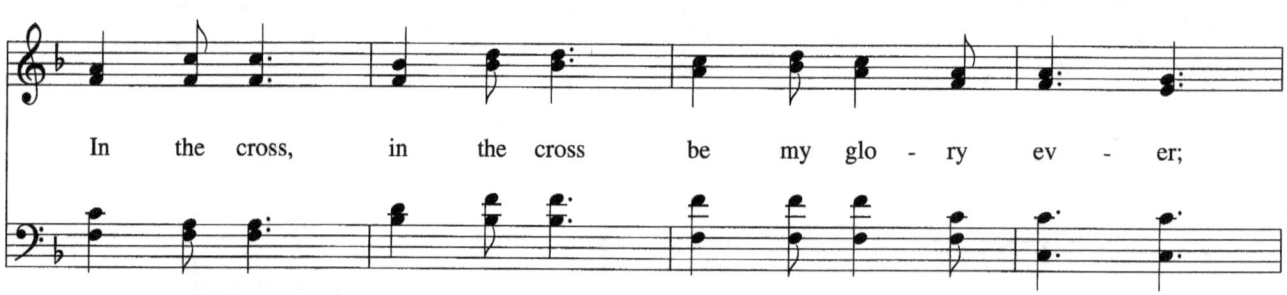

In the cross, in the cross be my glory ever;

till my raptured soul shall find rest beyond the river.

Near the Cross
(The hymn as played)

Piano

arr. Carl MaultsBy
© 2001 Malted Milk Music

On Christ the Solid Rock *(The hymn as written)*

Words: Edward Mote
Music: William B. Bradbury

30

On Christ the Solid Rock
(The hymn as played)

arr. Carl MaultsBy
© 2001 Malted Milk Music

This page intentionally left blank to facilitate page turns.

Come, Ye Disconsolate *(The hymn as written)*

Words: Stanza 1–2. Thomas Moore
       Stanza 3. Thomas Hasting

Music: Samuel Webbe

Come, Ye Disconsolate
(The hymn as played)

Piano

arr. Carl MaultsBy
© 2001 Malted Milk Music

♩. = 48

This page intentionally left blank to facilitate page turns.

When We All Get to Heaven *(The hymn as written)*

Words: Eliza Edmunds Hewitt
Music: Emily Divine Wilson

1. Sing the wondrous love of Jesus, sing His mercy and His grace;
   in the mansion bright and blessed, He'll prepare for us a place.
2. While we walk the pilgrim pathway, clouds will overspread the sky;
   but when trav'ling days are over, not a shadow, not a sigh.
3. Let us then be true and faithful, trusting, serving ev'ry day;
   just one glimpse of Him in glory will the toils of life repay.
4. Onward to the prize before us! Soon His beauty we'll behold;
   soon the pearly gates will open; we shall tread the streets of gold.

Refrain:
When we all get to heaven, what a day of rejoicing that will be!
When we all see Jesus, we'll sing and shout the victory.

When We All Get To Heaven
(The hymn as played)

Piano

arr. Carl MaultsBy
© 2001 Malted Milk Music

We're Marching to Zion *(The hymn as written)*

Words: Isaac Watts

Music: Robert S. Lowry

1. Come, we that love the Lord, and let our joys be known; join in a song with sweet accord, join in a song with sweet accord, and thus surround the throne, and thus surround the throne.
2. Let those refuse to sing who never knew our God; but children of the heav'nly King, but children of the heav'nly King, may speak their joys abroad, may speak their joys abroad.
3. The hill of Zion yields a thousand sacred sweets before we reach the heav'nly fields, before we reach the heav'nly fields, or walk the golden streets, or walk the golden streets.
4. Then let our songs abound, and ev'ry tear be dry; we're marching through Immanuel's ground, we're marching thro' Immanuel's ground, to fairer worlds on high, to fairer worlds on high.

We're marching to Zion, beautiful, beautiful Zion; we're marching upward to Zion, the beautiful city of God.

Zion, Zion,

This Little Light Of Mine
(The hymn as played)

arr. Carl MaultsBy
© 2001 Malted Milk Music

There Is a Fountain *(The hymn as written)*

Words: William Cowper

Music: American Melody
arr. Lowell Mason

There Is A Fountain
(The hymn as played)

arr. Carl MaultsBy
© 2001 Malted Milk Music

Leaning on the Everlasting Arms *(The hymn as written)*

Words: Elisha A. Hoffman

Music: Anthony J. Showalter
arr. Carl Haywood from *Songs of Praise*

46

47

Leaning on the Everlasting Arms
(The hymn as played)

Piano   arr. Carl MaultsBy
© 2001 Malted Milk Music

This page intentionally left blank to facilitate page turns.

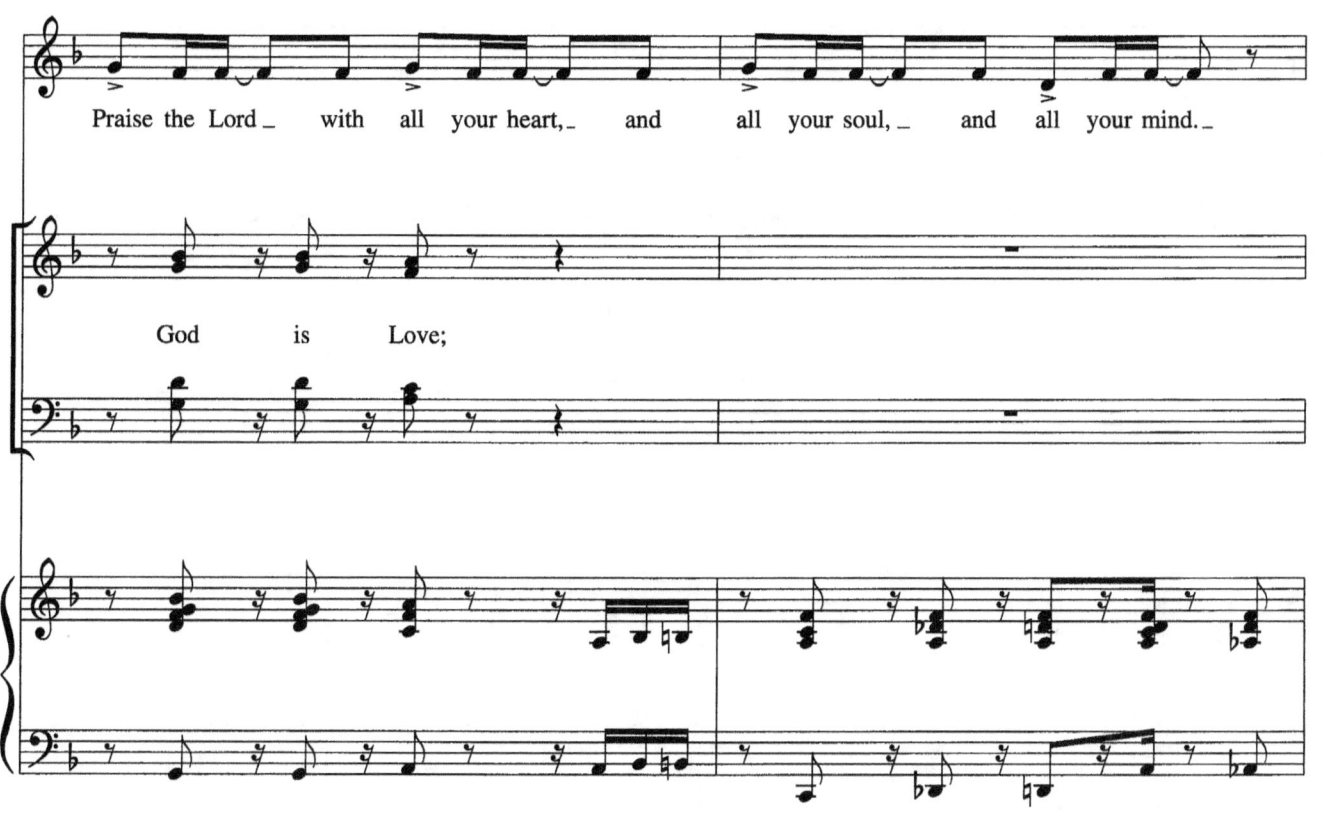

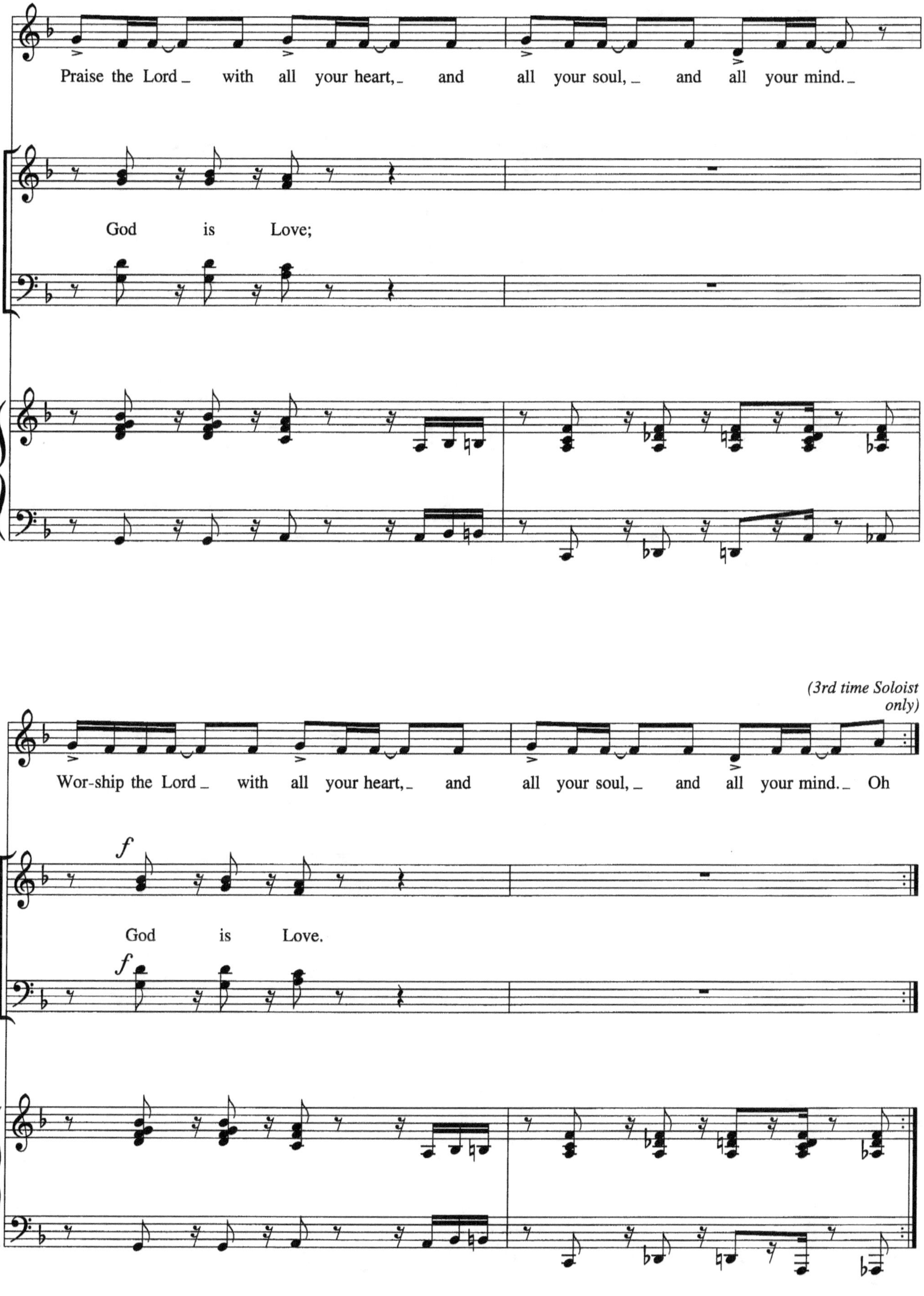
Praise the Lord with all your heart, and all your soul, and all your mind.
God is Love;
(3rd time Soloist only)
Wor-ship the Lord with all your heart, and all your soul, and all your mind. Oh
God is Love.

www.ingramcontent.com/pod-product-compliance
Lightning Source LLC
Chambersburg PA
CBHW082143230426
43672CB00016B/2940